Michael Mitrović
Michael Schuster

Meteora between heaven and earth

Bibliografische Information der Deutschen Nationalbibliothek:
Die Deutsche Nationalbibliothek verzeichnet diese Publikation
in der Deutschen Nationalbibliografie; detaillierte bibliografische
Daten sind im Internet über dnb.dnb.de abrufbar.

© 2019
Michael Mitrović
Michael Schuster
Translation into English by Benjamin Mitrović
Original title: Meteora – zwischen Himmel und Erde, © 2018

Herstellung und Verlag:
BoD – Books on Demand, Norderstedt
ISBN: 978-3-7460-8124-3

It has been many long years ago, when I decided to visit for the first time the Meteora monasteries and, like most tourists, planned to visit with only one night's stay – that makes two full days!

And like everyone who experiences for the first time this unique landscape, combined with the perception of the strong faith of the orthodox church, I was fascinated, speechless, inspired.

I wandered exclusively on asphalt roads to as many monasteries as was possible in that short span of time (I think it were five). During the descent on the evening of the second day I came upon a signpost with the inscription: "Μονή Βαρλαάμ" and a deep yearning took hold of me to walk this solitary footpath.

Unfortunately there didn't remain time for that!

My inner yearning accumulated over the span of ten years. Then I set out for the second time to explore the world of the Meteora landscape, this time staying for five days.

Since then, each year I spend many days there, visiting multiple times. The landscape, the monasteries, the people have called to me…

M. M.

Kalabaka

A microcosm at the feet of the Meteora cliffs,
though still young in years
in comparison to the ancient rocks,
it was already known to the Romans,
to the geographer Strabon
as Aiginion,
later it was called Stagoi,
finally rechristened as Kalabaka by the Turks.
The upper city is surmounted
by the byzantine chapel
the Assumption of the Virgin Mary.
The lower city is bustling with activity,
all the time reverently watched over
by the monastery Agios Stefanos.

Footpaths

How can one approach
the monastic seclusion
of the Meteora?
Certainly not with the tourist bus
along the asphalt road
in all but ten minutes to the peak.
One has to humbly go step by step,
by way of Kalabaka or way of Kastraki.
With each step uphill one becomes calmer,
pious, amazed and foreboding...
On solitary mountain paths
piece by piece one leaves
the world behind oneself...
One immerses oneself
in God's Cradle
between heaven and earth...

Kastraki

Founded by a people
who were escaping from the Turks,
Kastraki evolved to becoming a place of transit
to the Meteora monasteries.
The cottages of the upper city
wistfully seem to nestle themselves
into the rocky cliffs,
as if to claim their part
of the monastic salvation.
Between the Spindel and the Doupiani chapel
as well as the ruins of the monastery of the Holy Ghost
and that of the Holy Nikolaos of Bandova
the village receives its particular blessing.

The Spindel

In the church square of Kastraki
one's sight is magically drawn
to the Spindel high above,
placed there by divine dispensation.
From this peak a spiritual line of force emanates
to the very location where later
the chapel and the village were founded.
The spirituality that emanates from the Spindel
has been present here since ancient times,
well before the Church and Christianity.
It stands erect like an exclamation mark!
Its spectacle radiates power and security.
The ascension goes along well-trodden paths
past two old little churches.

The Doupiani Chapel

This small old chapel
is crouched timidly
at the entrance to the valley
of the Meteora monasteries,
it is nestled closely
into the Doupiani cliffs.
All monks on a pilgrimage
of their calling
passed by this place,
a spiritual transit,
and continued on with newfound resolve
and inner fortitude!

Ex oriente lux – from the east originates the light

In the morning, shortly after sunrise, there is complete silence.
The rock formations reside here as they have for millennia.
And as is rite since hundreds of years
the monks and nuns
in the monastery chapels
have congregated hours before in the middle of night,
to celebrate the holy liturgy.
Standing outside one can't hear their chanting.
One stands at the feet of the cliffs
in the small village of Kastraki and looks above.
From this location we can see four monasteries:
Varlaam, Metamorfosis, Roussanou and Nikolaos Anapavsas.
And a bird of prey that quietly circles around the rock formations.
In the inner sanctum of the holy monasteries the miracle unfolds -
to thavma – the orthodox worship.
Those with ears to listen,
and eyes to see,
witness God's miracle,
the miracle of existence,
even from outside the monastery walls...

Exterior and interior truth

It is difficult to resolve the question
of what is more astonishing,
the monastic life of the Meteora
or its surrounding beauty of nature.
Probably it is the unique symbiosis of both these traits
that manifests itself here.
The first solitary monks
started to settle here,
because they were overwhelmed
by the seclusion and beauty
of this place.
And in return, with their presence
and the construction of their monasteries,
they have further refined
the beauty of this place!

Between heaven and earth

Our sight is magically drawn
to the most remote places
on rocky ledges, on plateaus, at the edge of slopes,
seemingly floating in the heavens, carried by the clouds -
and it is here that we behold the monasteries
or their remains and ruins.
And immediately one realizes:
whoever constructed these buildings by the sweat of their brow
to praise God and Jesus Christ,
must have deeply immersed oneself
in the miracle of orthodoxy.

Perpetual light

The lighting in the cliffs of the Meteora monasteries
always seems somewhat unreal,
regardless of the weather conditions.
For we behold the objects of our corporal realm
not only with our physical eyes,
but furthermore with our introversive senses.
And the objects make themselves seen to us
not only in their physical likeness,
but coinstantaneous they also exude
states of ethereal condition.
Thus comes into being the enchantment of light and shape,
of ether and force,
of volition and effect...

The wisdom of nature

The actual devoutness
during the ascension up the mountains
originates from nature.
The bustling twittering of the birds,
the bleeping and warbling,
the vivacious flight from branch to branch,
the majestic floating
high above around the cliffs.
The morning tranquility.
Hopefully no tourist will cross my path.
He would disturb the holy simplicity.
The ever-greening shrubs and bushes.
Then suddenly in the distance
the slow gliding flight of a stork.
It carries the wisdom from the earth to the heavens.
It has built its nest
on top of the chapel dome -
a safe place.

The center of force

Each time anew,
when I traverse the landscape
of the Meteora monasteries,
I feel this great wondrousness,
an overpowering, a speechlessness -
as if I was here for the very first time.
From the rock formations radiates some
otherworldly force and energy,
that occupies and affects everything around it.
Time and time again
I stand awestruck
in front of particular cliffs or chasms,
and at the same time in front of the complete ensemble.
Here lies hidden a center of force of the earth.
The monks have divined it,
many hundred years ago...

On the path uphill

A mountain climbing party in the cliff side.
Where are they headed?
To the summit?
What are they holding on to?
To the rocks, to their ropes?
What do they want to achieve?
To conquer the most difficult route
as quickly as possible?
I see them
like pearls on a string.
Contacting each other along the rope.
From the topmost climber
a rope reaches into the heavens
... securing the whole of society...

Images of the saints

So many tourists hurry past,
with loud voices and
readied cameras or smartphones!
So few take the time
to contemplate the image of the saint.
The subdued and yet pervasive colors.
The meek facial expression of the Virgin Mary.
The innocent looking infant Jesus.
Even people not of orthodox belief
can easily surmise how deeply the artist
must have been rooted in tradition
that created this image!

Liturgy

Liturgy in the ancient byzantine church.
The walls draped with holy icons.
Almost exclusively older people are present,
a few middle aged women,
one even with her little daughter.
Most carry a candle in hand,
which they have lit.
Upon entering the room,
they kiss one or several
especially precious icons.
During most of the liturgy they stand on their feet.
Certainly the sanctity arises
not only from the presence of the people.
It is the location, the time of Easter,
and the popes commemorating the liturgy,
that remind us of this miracle.
After forty minutes I take
my share of devoutness outside.
Shortly thereafter I sit in the rain
for ninety minutes under some overhanging rock.
This is then the continuation
of the liturgy...

Reunion with Varlaam

The ascension to the monastery of Varlaam.
Finally I can heed my inner calling.
Many years ago I discovered an unremarkable wooden sign
with the name of this monastery on it.
The path seemed all too compelling,
even, as a kind of spiritual quest,
outright necessary.
But I didn't have the time then,
my departure was imminent.
Many years passed by.
Now the time has come.
They are humble, reflective steps,
that I walk slowly.
On this narrow path probably thousands of monks
have pilgrimaged to the top before me,
(whose skulls lie neatly lined up in the charnel house even today)
in a time when cars didn't yet exist.
Freedom fighters travelled this path as well,
in their struggle against the Turks,
and later against the German occupants...
In this moment now the path belongs to me alone,
me and my thoughts and perceptions...

Varlaam

Along the old footpath from Kastraki
across the market place,
through the vineyards,
by way of the chapel of the Holy Georg,
past the Dragoncave,
through the monastery garden,
sitting in a net, confiding in God
and the monk brotherhood,
with human labor hoisted up by a winch,
later, in prayer
in front of the richly decorated wall of icons,
bemused by the incense,
Lord be praised– Kyrie Eleison!

The prison of the monks

Behind wooden bars with only water and bread,
motivated to humility and penance,
in perpetual conversation with God,
asking for remission of their sins,
exposed to the elements,
a vantage point to the Dragoncave...
For what reason do the monks languish here?
We don't know!
They are reasons wholly human...

The Dragoncave

Once in distant memory,
when dragons still existed
and there were no church or monks,
no streets or houses,
one such beast roamed
the Meteora mountains
and kept vigil,
that no evil energies
would make this land uninhabitable.
When the monks arrived
and built their monasteries,
the dragon recognized
that everything was as it should be.
Therefore he moved on to other lands,
where he was needed more urgently.
His cave can be visited even today.

Metamorfosis

The biggest monastery of them all,
sitting enthroned on the highest peak,
the meaning of its name: transformation.
The view wanders from the Pinios valley
to the nearby Pindos mountains,
while on the other side
it follows along the rocky cliffs,
past the village of Kalabaka
to infinite plains beyond.
Not all that long ago,
when paved streets didn't yet exist,
nor motorized buses
that would carry the waves of tourists,
to get up here – or anywhere really –
one had to traverse along ladders and nets,
this was the only means
to reach the monastery.

Agia Triada

Nothing can be seen or heard
of the secular goings-on,
this high up on the mountain of the monastery
of the Holy Trinity.
Not the roister of the musicians
and carousers in the taverns...
Not the bustling activity in the market square...
Not the exultation over the winning soccer team...
Not the lamenting over the dead in the cemetery...
Nor the blaring of the cars...
All that can be heard
is the infinite trickle of time,
a divine ambient noise at the edge of the world,
spherical chimes from the heavens,
a susurrant singing
in the hour of night...

Eaglerock surmounting the village

On the narrow Eaglerock,
in the likeness of God's finger,
of all the monasteries
maybe the closest one to the heavens?
And at the same time
the one most attached
to Kalabaka,
with its view
from the conventual cliffs
far across the plains,
up to the opposite mountain range.
The village lays
at its feet.
Standing above at the cross,
carefully listening,
one can clearly perceive
the sounds of the daily routine,
so close – and yet so far away...

Clouds

Cloud veiled monasteries,
a misty day.
The order of worldly events
do not perturb the clouds.
Prayers, liturgies
are conducted in a strict pattern,
the secular world outside
is of no concern in this regard.
„Lord, have mercy on us!"
chant or pray
the monks and nuns
inside the monastery.
To this, most visitors
turn a deaf ear.

Roussanou

Mistress of the valley to Kastraki,
and the gateway to Metamorfosis,
a marvel between heaven and earth,
a rock cliff, surrounded by more cliffs.
Looking above one catches sight of Varlaam,
downwards of the monastery Nikolaos Anapavsas.
Up here the soul feels
weightless.
To the visitor it is difficult
to return to his everyday life.

Agios Nikolaos

This is the very first monastery
that catches the eye of the wanderer,
coming by way of Kastraki.
Defiantly sitting enthroned on a narrow cliff,
unconquerable.
Within, precious mural paintings,
heralding the deep beliefs
of our forefathers.
Outside, at the highest peak,
sitting beneath the bell tower,
a wonderful spot,
one seems to be floating
on a tiny cloud.

Agios Stefanos

Once, returning from a hike
through the Koziakas mountains,
seeing the Meteora cliffs from a distance,
my sight was magically drawn
to the monastery of Agios Stefanos.
And though I was weary already,
after several hours of hiking,
I felt this strong urge
to pilgrimage
right now
to this very monastery.
Only having reached the top,
did my inner tranquility return.
Agios Stefanos doesn't exude its full impression
when looking above
from Kalabaka,
but rather when watching from a distance.
It is then, that one feels the full extent of its allurement!

Daily routine

The locals don't notice it anymore.
When one is fed delicious foods
every day of the year,
one quickly loses the exquisite taste of it.
But to those of us who only dwell
in this place for a limited time,
the monasteries constantly watch over us,
though silently and from down here invisibly
(except for one!),
but ever-present.
It is as if
the holy Meteora monasteries
bestowed a particular radiance, an aura,
to the human settlements
at their feet.
All one has to do,
is to get involved with these delicate vibrations,
to become a part of the whole.

The Organ Pipes

Just a few steps up the mountain
past the monasteries of Metamorfosis and Varlaam
the often frantic tourist sounds lapse into silence.
The sudden peace and quiet
and the long view across the Pinios river
towards the Pindos mountains
take the wanderers breath away.
In the distance sheep silently blare.
If one is extra quiet,
maybe spherical tones can be heard,
emanating from the Organ Pipes,
intoned in ancient times.
Who possesses nowadays the faculty
to play such an instrument?
In a time when we have need
of divine sounds more than ever?

The secluded monastery Ipapantis

During the descent on the far side
of the big monastery,
past the Organ Pipes,
it is only at the very last moment
that one beholds, hewn into the rock,
the secluded monastery Ipapantis.
At all times the monks have felt the urge
to live in caves and rocks,
distant from time and worldly affairs.
The foundation may be inhospitable,
certainly,
but it is made
for eternity.

The figurine of the freedom fighter

On the upper side
of the secluded monastery Ipapantis,
on a plateau leading into the valley
the statue of the freedom fighter
of Vlachava
keeps vigil on his pedestal.
To the sorely afflicted people,
once again in our modern times,
bestowing encouragement,
instilling them with hope.
A bulwark against the Ottomans and Huns,
a warrior clad in God's garment.

Ruins

What the visitor can see
of the monasteries nowadays,
is only a fraction
of what our forefathers had built.
Many monastery ruins, foundations,
tower stumps, overgrown architecture
bear witness of this.
Behold, to what steep locations
they boldly and dauntlessly climbed
to accomplish their deed.
And even though the ever prevailing evanescence,
the passing of time, the might of the elements
destroyed most everything,
all too human,
there still remains posthumously
a distant echo of eternity.

The River

Past Kalabaka the river Pinios
runs into the valley,
seemingly unremarkable,
shallow in summer time,
but powerful and torrential
in spring when the ice melts.
Many small streams
from the surrounding mountains
flow into the river,
at many places covered with age-old trees,
traversed by daringly winding bridges,
constructed by Turkish craftsmen.
Gushing springs and waterfalls
are plentiful
in this blessed land.

Ancient Trees

Ancient trees at the course of the stream,
defying the passage of time.
What all have they seen?
How many people have passed them by?
With good or with bad intentions.
Landmarks and protectors from storms,
shade-giving and offering shelter for animals.
Already our fathers and forefathers
have known them,
may our children's children still
be able to delight in them!

The Icon

Maria with the infant Jesus,
the embodiment
of maternal benevolence,
in her arms she carries
the coming savior,
a perpetual promise
for peace on earth.
Hope, faith, assurance.
The holy icon
invites us
to immersion and meditation.
In the orthodox church
it is an object
of the greatest veneration.

Towards Heaven

The ways of the Lord are unforeseeable,
the ways of humans often arduous.
Faith can move mountains,
we are told,
always there are ups and downs in life.
It is good indeed then,
if one's view is directed upwards
and we are lead
by an unflinching faith.

Further Information about Meteora
under the following link:

http://www.salinos.de/links/meteora.php